How to Build Credit Fast Without Debt

Step-by-Step Guide to Boost Your Credit Score Fast Using Rent, Utilities, and Secured Cards—No Loans, No Interest, No Debt

By Joe Correa

Published by Live Stronger Faster

This book is for educational and informational purposes only. The author and publisher are not engaged in rendering legal, financial, or other professional advice. Readers should consult a qualified professional before making any financial decisions.

First Edition

TABLE OF CONTENTS

INTRODUCTION

Let's get one thing straight: you do **not** need debt to build great credit.

That myth has kept millions of people stuck in a cycle of borrowing, paying interest, and hoping their credit score will magically improve over time. It's a broken system that rewards banks, not individuals. And it's time for something better.

That's why I created this book.

Whether you're just starting out with zero credit, trying to recover from past mistakes, or simply looking for a smarter way to boost your score, this guide will show you how to do it **fast**, **safely**, and most importantly—**without going into debt**.

I've worked with thousands of people who believed they had no shot at building credit without loans. But once they followed this system, they watched their scores climb—sometimes by 50, 100, even 150 points in a matter of months. And they did it without borrowing a dollar.

This book is your step-by-step blueprint to do the same.

Who This Is For?

This book is designed for people who want to build or rebuild their credit **without interest, loans, or risk**. It's especially powerful for:

- Young adults with no credit history

- Students who want to build credit before graduation
- Immigrants who are new to the U.S. credit system
- Entrepreneurs preparing for future funding
- Parents and professionals recovering from past financial challenges
- Anyone who wants **control** over their credit without the stress of debt

If you've ever been denied a lease, rejected for a card, or embarrassed by a low score—even when you're financially responsible—this book is for you.

You'll finally understand how the credit system works, what it's really measuring, and how to reverse-engineer a high score using tools you already have access to.

What You'll Learn

In the chapters ahead, you'll learn how to:

- Establish your first credit score with no cosigner
- Add your rent, utilities, and streaming services to your report
- Use secured credit cards and builder accounts *without* paying interest
- Track and grow your score in 30, 60, and 90-day stages
- Avoid costly mistakes that sabotage thousands of people every year
- Leverage other people's credit—safely and ethically
- Maintain a 700+ score without touching a loan

We'll also look at real-life stories from people who went from **invisible** to **credit-approved**, using the same strategies you're about to learn.

This book is full of tools, checklists, and examples you can apply immediately—even if you're starting from zero.

What This Book Is Not

This is not a get-rich-quick scheme.
It's not about hacking the system with shady tricks.
And it's definitely not about borrowing your way to a better score.

This book is about **empowerment**.

It's about learning to play the game of credit the *right* way, so you win long-term—not just for your next apartment or card, but for your future home, business, or investment opportunity.

You don't need to borrow thousands.
You don't need a perfect job.
You don't need to wait years to improve your credit.

You just need a plan. And you're holding it.

Why Credit Without Debt Is the Smart Way Forward

For years, the credit industry pushed the lie that borrowing equals building.

That's not just misleading—it's dangerous.

People get credit cards "just to build credit," then end up carrying balances, missing payments, and watching their scores crash. Others take out small loans they don't need, pay interest for months, and gain just a few points on their report.

That's not smart. That's expensive.

In this book, we flip the model.

You'll learn how to use **what you already pay for**—rent, subscriptions, bills—to build real credit history. You'll learn how to make banks and bureaus **recognize your financial behavior** without putting your money at risk.

And you'll do it in a way that's sustainable, repeatable, and safe.

Let's Build

So, take a breath. You're not behind. You're not disqualified. And you're definitely not the only one who's been confused or frustrated by credit.

By the end of this book, you'll:

- Know exactly what affects your credit score
- Have a simple 3-phase system to follow
- Understand how to grow your score fast without using debt
- And most importantly—feel confident in your financial future

Let's build your credit the right way.

Let's build it **fast**.

Let's build it **without debt**.

Your credit comeback starts now.

CHAPTER 1: THE FAST LANE TO CREDIT GROWTH WITHOUT RISK

Most people believe the only way to build credit is by going into debt.

That was certainly what 27-year-old Andrea believed when she sat across from her bank's credit advisor, nervously clutching a brochure that promised to "improve your credit score fast!" The fine print told a different story—12-month personal loan, 22.5% interest, and a monthly payment she could barely afford on her $38,000 salary as a freelance photographer.

Andrea had always been financially cautious. Raised by immigrant parents who paid cash for everything, she avoided credit cards and took pride in staying debt-free. But when she decided to rent a nicer apartment and her application was denied because of her "thin credit file," her confidence took a hit.

That moment was a wake-up call. She had done everything right—saved money, avoided debt, paid bills on time—but none of it showed up on a credit report. She was invisible to the credit system.

As Andrea scrolled through blogs and videos late into the night, she kept hearing the same advice: get a credit card, take out a loan, finance a purchase. But each suggestion felt like a trap. Was there no way to build credit without taking on risk?

Then she stumbled upon something different—a community forum of people who had built their credit without loans, interest, or debt of any kind. She read story after story of people using tools like rent reporting services, phone bill subscriptions, and secured accounts to grow their scores.

Her curiosity turned to hope.

Andrea started small. She signed up for a rent reporting service that added 18 months of on-time rent payments to her credit report. Next, she linked her Netflix and phone bills through a free credit reporting tool. She even applied for a credit builder account that held her savings in a locked certificate while reporting payments each month.

In just 90 days, her credit score jumped 70 points.

But what surprised her most wasn't the score boost—it was the sense of control. For the first time, she understood how credit worked. She wasn't relying on debt to prove her worth. She was building a financial identity on her own terms.

Six months later, Andrea applied for a rewards credit card and was approved instantly. She used it for gas and groceries—never carrying a balance—and watched her score continue to rise. When she finally applied again for that apartment, the leasing manager nodded, impressed by her 745 score.

"This is one of the best applications I've seen all month," he said.

Andrea smiled—not because she was proud of the number, but because she earned it without sacrificing her values.

Her story is not an exception.

Every day, thousands of people are rewriting the credit rulebook. They're ditching the myth that you need to go into debt to build credit, and they're doing it faster, safer, and smarter than ever before.

In this book, you're going to learn exactly how.

You'll discover the tools Andrea used—plus a few others you've probably never heard of. You'll learn how to track your progress, avoid common traps, and create a system that works for your lifestyle, your income, and your goals.

Most importantly, you'll learn how to build credit fast... without ever going into debt.

Because in today's world, the best financial power move isn't just having a high credit score—it's knowing you earned it without compromising your future.

Let's get started.

CHAPTER 2: CREDIT MYTHS—WHY YOU DON'T NEED DEBT TO BUILD CREDIT

If you're listening to this book, chances are you've heard at least one of these credit myths—and maybe even believed them. Don't worry. You're not alone. These myths are deeply rooted in our culture and pushed by banks, credit card companies, and even well-meaning friends and family.

But today, we're breaking them down—and more importantly, I'll show you step-by-step how to take smarter actions that actually work.

Myth #1: You Have to Borrow Money to Build Credit

Truth: You need credit activity—not debt.

Most people think borrowing money and carrying a balance is necessary to build credit. That's false.

Step 1: Open an account that reports to the credit bureaus without requiring debt.
Options include:

- Rent reporting services
- Experian Boost (adds utilities and streaming services)
- Credit builder savings accounts (your money is locked and released later)

These accounts report **positive payment history** without requiring you to borrow anything.

Result: You build credit with payments you're already making—zero interest, zero risk.

Myth #2: You Need to Carry a Balance to Boost Your Score

Truth: Carrying a balance can hurt your score and your wallet.

This myth costs Americans billions every year. Credit card companies love it because it means interest charges.

Step 2: Use your card and pay it off in full every month.

- Pay on or before the **statement date**, not just the due date, to lower your utilization ratio.
- Keep usage under **10%** of your credit limit if possible.

Example: If your limit is $500, try not to let your balance exceed $50 when it reports.

Result: You prove you're responsible without paying interest or risking debt.

Myth #3: You Need a Cosigner or a Loan to Start Credit

Truth: You can build independently with the right starter tools.

Step 3: Apply for a secured card or credit-building account with your own money.

- Secured cards are backed by a deposit (usually $200+).
- Some fintech platforms offer "credit lines" against your bank balance or savings.

Bonus Tip: Look for cards that graduate to unsecured after a few months of on-time payments.

Result: You build credit in your name without co-signers or loans.

Myth #4: All Debt Helps Your Score

Truth: Not all debt is treated equally—and some hurts more than it helps.

- Personal loans don't always improve your mix and can increase your debt-to-income ratio.
- High-interest or short-term debt (like payday loans) can tank your score if mismanaged.

Step 4: Avoid unnecessary debt in the name of "building credit."

Focus on the **three credit pillars** instead:

1. On-time payments
2. Low utilization
3. Age of accounts

Result: Your score rises steadily without risking financial setbacks.

Myth #5: You Need a High Income to Have Good Credit

Truth: Credit is about behavior, not income.

People with modest incomes can have excellent credit by simply being consistent.

Step 5: Automate your payments.

- Set up autopay on any reporting accounts.
- Use reminders to check your statement balances and report dates.
- Monitor your credit with free tools like Credit Karma, Experian, or NerdWallet.

Result: You don't have to be rich to build strong credit—you just need a system.

Summary of Steps to Break the Myths and Start Building Without Debt

1. Open reporting accounts that don't require borrowing.
2. Use your card and pay in full—avoid interest traps.

3. Start with a secured card or credit builder tool, not a loan.

4. Skip "fake credit builders" like payday loans or unnecessary loans.

5. Automate your credit behavior and track progress.

By following these steps, you're not just ignoring bad advice—you're building a smarter, stronger foundation for long-term credit success.

Why You Don't Need Debt to Build Credit

When Malik graduated college, he didn't have a job lined up—but he had ambition, a laptop, and a beat-up Honda Civic that could get him to every freelance gig he could find. What he didn't have was credit.

He hadn't taken out student loans, never had a credit card, and his parents always told him debt was dangerous. So when he went to apply for his first apartment, he was stunned to hear his application was denied.

"Sorry," the leasing agent told him. "You don't have any credit history. We need something to show you're responsible with payments."

Confused and embarrassed, Malik walked out of the office and sat in his car. How could he be penalized for *not* owing anyone money?

Later that night, he called his cousin Jasmine, who worked in real estate and finance. "You've got to get some credit activity going," she explained. "Not debt—activity. You need to show the bureaus something."

"But everyone says you have to borrow to build credit," he replied.

"Total myth," she said. "Let me show you how I built mine without a single loan."

Over the next week, Malik followed Jasmine's advice.

First, he signed up for a rent reporting service that let him submit his monthly rent payments from his current sublease. Even though his landlord wasn't part of a big company, the service verified and submitted his on-time payments to the credit bureaus.

Then, he opened a free credit reporting tool that added his phone bill and Spotify account to his credit profile. "You're already paying those," Jasmine said. "Now they'll help your score."

He was skeptical. "That simple?"

"That simple."

Next, Jasmine suggested a secured card. Malik took $200 from his savings and opened one with a company that reported to all three credit bureaus. He set a reminder in his phone: *Use for gas only. Pay off before the statement date*. No balance, no interest, no debt.

He made sure to stay under $20 of use each month—just enough to show activity but low enough to keep his credit utilization below 10%.

At first, Malik didn't think much of it. But three months later, he got an alert: his credit score had gone from 0 to 689.

He stared at the screen in disbelief. "Wait... I didn't borrow anything!"

He logged into the rent portal, the card app, and the reporting tool—and sure enough, everything had been reporting cleanly. On-time payments, low utilization, active accounts. All without a dime of debt.

He called Jasmine that night, nearly shouting. "Why isn't this stuff taught in school?"

"Because schools don't get referral commissions from credit card companies," she laughed. "But now *you* know."

A few months later, Malik went back to that same apartment complex. This time, the leasing agent smiled. "Nice credit score—you're approved."

And when Malik finally had a steady income and started to think about buying a car, he didn't need a cosigner or a high-interest loan. His credit report told a story of responsibility, not risk.

Now, Malik teaches his younger siblings the same truth: You don't need to borrow money to build credit. You just need to understand the game—and play it with strategy.

Because the real myth isn't that you need debt to build credit. The real myth is believing you're powerless without it.

CHAPTER 3: CREDIT BUILDER TOOLS THAT DON'T REQUIRE BORROWING

Diana was a single mom with two kids and a full-time job as a medical assistant. After her divorce, her finances were tight—but she was determined to rebuild her life, including her credit.

There was just one problem: she didn't want to go into debt to do it.

Years ago, she'd made that mistake—maxing out credit cards during hard times, paying the minimums, and watching interest charges grow like weeds. She'd worked hard to pay everything off, and the idea of getting back into that cycle made her stomach turn.

But when her oldest son needed a new laptop for school, she realized she needed access to credit again—just in case. The trouble was, she hadn't used credit in years. Her score was low, her file was thin, and her confidence was shaky.

So, Diana did what she always did when she needed answers: she made a list.

She wrote across the top:
How to Build Credit Without Borrowing Money.

The first item on her list came from a friend who worked in property management:
1. Report Rent Payments to Credit Bureaus.

She had always paid rent on time, but none of it had ever been reported. So she signed up with a rent reporting service. They contacted her landlord, verified her last 24 months of on-time rent, and sent the full history to TransUnion and Equifax. Within weeks, her score went up nearly 40 points.

She was amazed. "I've been paying rent for 10 years," she told her friend. "Why didn't anyone tell me I could get credit for it?"

Next, she checked off item two:
2. Use Your Bills to Boost Credit.

Diana found a free service that linked her bank account and added recurring payments—like her cell phone, water bill, Netflix, and electric bill—to her Experian credit report. These were bills she already paid monthly. Now, they finally counted for something.

Then came number three:
3. Open a Credit Builder Savings Account.

This one felt odd at first. She deposited $25 a month into a locked savings account. She couldn't touch the money until the term ended—but each "payment" was reported as an on-time installment to all three bureaus.

It was a reverse loan—*she* was the lender. But the credit system saw her as someone successfully repaying a loan, and her score ticked upward again.

Number four made her nervous:
4. Use a Secured Credit Card—Cautiously.

Diana used $250 of her tax refund to open a secured card. She promised herself she would use it for one thing only: groceries.

Every month, she used no more than $50 and paid it off before the due date. Her utilization stayed low, and she never paid a cent in interest. Six months later, her card company offered to graduate her to an unsecured card—and refunded her deposit.

Finally, she added one more step to her system:

5. Monitor and Automate Everything.

She downloaded a free app that tracked her credit score, gave her alerts, and reminded her of reporting dates. She set every bill and card on auto-pay and checked in once a week to make sure everything stayed on track.

By the end of the year, Diana's score had climbed 112 points. She had no loans, no balances, and no interest payments—just a clean credit report full of smart activity.

Her friends were stunned when she told them.

"Wait, you didn't borrow anything?" one asked.

"Nope," Diana smiled. "I just figured out how to play the game without losing."

Her journey became the blueprint for her sister, her coworkers, and even her 16-year-old son—who was already asking how he could start early.

These are the same tools available to you right now:

Quick Recap: Tools That Build Credit Without Borrowing

- **Rent reporting services** (like RentTrack or Boom)
- **Utility and subscription reporting tools** (like Experian Boost)

- **Credit builder savings accounts** (like Self or CreditStrong)
- **Secured credit cards with no annual fee**
- **Free credit monitoring tools and automation apps**

You don't need to go into debt to build credit. You need activity, consistency, and tools designed for people who want to grow without risk.

Just like Diana, you can use what you already have—your rent, your bills, your habits—and turn them into credit strength. No loans required.

In the next chapter, we'll take this even further by showing you how to **use rent, subscriptions, and bills in combination** to maximize your credit score gains in just a few months.

You've got the tools. Let's use them with strategy.

CHAPTER 4: USING RENT, SUBSCRIPTIONS, AND BILLS TO BOOST SCORES

Tyrese had been working two jobs—daytime delivery driver and weekend DJ—for nearly five years. He had a good reputation with everyone he worked with. Never late. Always professional. But when he applied for a car loan to replace his aging, 2004 sedan, the bank gave him a short, painful answer:

> "We can't approve this loan because you have an insufficient credit profile."

He stared at the rejection email for a while. "Insufficient?" he muttered. "I pay rent, phone, water, lights... What else do they want?"

That frustration turned into fuel.

Tyrese wasn't going to let an invisible score define his future. He decided to treat his credit like a business. Step one? Research.

He started watching YouTube videos, reading articles, and listening to podcasts. The same tip kept coming up: **You're already making payments that could build your credit—you just need to report them.**

So he grabbed a notebook, drew a line down the middle, and titled one side: **Monthly Bills I Pay.**
On the other side: **Which Ones Can Be Reported?**

Here's what his list looked like:

Left column – Monthly Bills

- Rent: $1,200
- Cell phone: $75
- Internet: $60
- Netflix: $15
- Electricity: $110
- Water: $40
- Car insurance: $135

Right column – Reportable?

- Rent: YES
- Cell phone: YES
- Internet: YES
- Netflix: YES
- Electricity: YES
- Water: YES
- Car insurance: MAYBE (depends on provider)

He realized he was spending nearly $1,600 a month—but none of it was improving his credit score.

The next day, Tyrese signed up with a rent reporting company called **Boom**, which could report both past and future rent payments to the bureaus. They contacted his landlord, verified the lease, and within two weeks, Tyrese had 12 months of on-time rent payments added to his credit report.

He also enrolled in **Experian Boost**, which synced to his checking account and found recurring payments—like Netflix, his phone bill, and even internet—and added them to his credit history. It wasn't magic, but his score jumped 28 points in the first 30 days.

He was hooked.

Now that he had a system, Tyrese wanted to get the most out of every dollar. He called his utility companies and asked, "Do you report to the credit bureaus?" Most didn't, but he learned that services like **LevelCredit** and **Grow Credit** could link some utilities and even streaming services for reporting.

He signed up.

Next, he opened a separate checking account just for bills. That way, he could automate payments, prevent missed due dates, and keep clean records for reporting tools. This not only helped his credit—it helped his sanity.

After three months, Tyrese logged into Credit Karma and couldn't believe his eyes:

Credit score: 714

He took a screenshot and sent it to his mom.

"You did this without a credit card?" she asked.

"Yup," he replied. "Just turned my bills into assets."

His old mindset had been: *Pay bills and forget about it.*
His new mindset: *Every payment is a step toward financial leverage.*

And it was paying off.

Tyrese didn't stop there. He started telling everyone he worked with—especially other gig workers—how to use rent, subscriptions, and bills to build credit.

One of the DJs he trained was only 20 years old, with zero credit. Tyrese helped him set up the same strategy, and within 6 months, that kid was approved for his first apartment—without a cosigner.

Tyrese realized something powerful: credit isn't about borrowing. It's about behavior. And if you pay your bills consistently, you deserve credit for it.

Quick Story Takeaways: How Tyrese Did It

1. **Reported Rent:** Used Boom to report past and future rent.

2. **Used Experian Boost:** Added recurring subscriptions and phone bills.

3. **Used Additional Tools:** LevelCredit and Grow Credit added more utility and service payments.

4. **Opened a Bills Account:** Separated finances for easy tracking and automation.

5. **Watched His Score Climb:** 714 in 90 days—no debt, no loans, no interest.

CHAPTER 5: LEVERAGING AUTHORIZED USER ACCOUNTS SAFELY

Carlos had just turned 21 when he walked into his local credit union to apply for his first credit card. He was working part-time at an auto shop and going to trade school in the evenings. He wasn't looking for anything fancy—just a simple card to help him build his credit.

The bank clerk politely pulled up his file, looked at the screen, and sighed.

> "Carlos, I'm sorry. You have no credit history, so we can't issue a card at this time."

Carlos nodded, disappointed but not surprised. No credit meant no approval—but no approval meant no way to build credit. It felt like a trap.

That night, he talked to his older sister, Natalie, who had a solid financial track record and worked as a nurse. She had a credit score over 800 and used credit cards like a tool—always paying in full, never missing a payment.

Carlos explained what happened.
Natalie paused, then smiled. "You know, I think I can help you out."

She pulled out her wallet and tapped one of her cards.

> "I'll add you as an authorized user."

Carlos blinked. "Wait... I won't have to use it, right?"

"Nope. You don't even need to hold the card. I'll just add your name. My history becomes your history—at least on this account."

Carlos was skeptical. "Is that even allowed?"

Natalie laughed. "It's encouraged. Credit bureaus love seeing positive history—even if it comes from someone else. As long as I keep paying on time, your score goes up. But listen—this only works if we do it smart."

The Rules of the Game

Over the next hour, Natalie explained the rules:

- **Rule 1:** Only use a card with a long, clean history.
  Her card was over 5 years old with a $10,000 limit and 2% utilization.

- **Rule 2:** No missed payments—ever.
  A single late payment would tank *both* their scores.

- **Rule 3:** Carlos wouldn't use the card at all.
  It was purely a tool for reporting history—not for spending.

A few days later, Natalie added Carlos as an authorized user through her card's online portal. It was free. No credit check. No hassle.

Within 30 days, Carlos received an alert:

> "A new account has been added to your credit report."

And just like that, he had a 700+ credit score.

He couldn't believe it. One month ago, he had zero. Now, lenders would see five years of perfect payment history and low usage. All thanks to his sister's responsible habits.

Carlos didn't go on a spending spree. Instead, he followed Natalie's example. He opened a secured card of his own with a $300 deposit and used it only for gas. He paid it off weekly and kept his utilization below 10%.

By the end of the semester, Carlos applied again for a credit card—and was approved instantly, no deposit required.

The Power—and Risk—of Being an Authorized User

This strategy worked wonders for Carlos, but Natalie made sure he understood the risks:

> "If I mess up, your score drops. And if *you* mess up on your own cards later, no authorized user status will save you."

He also learned that not all credit cards report authorized users to all three bureaus. So, before she added him, Natalie confirmed that her card did report to **Equifax**, **TransUnion**, and **Experian**.

Carlos also learned to avoid two big mistakes people make with this strategy:

- **Adding someone you don't fully trust.**
  Natalie knew she could trust Carlos. But too many people add friends or boyfriends who rack up charges and disappear.

- **Being added to a bad account.**
  If someone has late payments, high balances, or a short

credit history, being added to their card can actually *lower* your score.

Using This Strategy the Right Way

Carlos shared the idea with a friend at school, David, who wanted to try it too. But David made a mistake—he asked his uncle to add him to a maxed-out store card with three late payments in the past year.

His score dropped 40 points.

Carlos told him what Natalie taught him:

> "It only works if the account is strong. Otherwise, you're better off building credit the slow way than damaging it with the fast way."

Key Takeaways from Carlos' Journey

1. **Choose the Right Person:** Must be financially responsible and have a long, clean history.

2. **Verify Reporting:** Not all credit cards report authorized users to all bureaus. Call and check first.

3. **Keep It Low Risk:** You don't need access to the card—just the history.

4. **Don't Abuse It:** Use the score boost to start your own credit, not to rack up debt.

5. **Be Prepared to Be Removed:** Once your credit is strong enough, ask to be removed to stand on your own.

This strategy isn't about shortcuts—it's about leverage.

Like Carlos, you can use someone else's history as a foundation—but your credit success depends on what you build on top of it.

In the next chapter, we'll explore the **differences between secured cards and alternative credit-building accounts**, so you can choose the best path forward depending on your income, comfort level, and long-term goals.

CHAPTER 6: SECURED CARDS VS. ALTERNATIVE CREDIT BUILDING ACCOUNTS

Emily was proud of how far she had come. Just two years earlier, she was stuck in a job she hated, living paycheck to paycheck with no savings, no credit, and no options.

Now, she had a steady income from her new bookkeeping side hustle, a modest emergency fund, and a clear goal: to buy a reliable car within the next six months—with financing in her name.

But when she checked her credit report, her score was still sitting in the mid-500s. No active accounts. Just a closed utility bill from years ago and a student loan marked as "paid in full." It wasn't bad—it just wasn't enough.

She needed new activity on her credit report.

So she did what most people do: opened a new browser tab and searched,

> "How to build credit fast with low risk."

Almost every article mentioned **secured credit cards**. But a few mentioned **credit builder accounts**, like Self and CreditStrong. Emily was torn. Which one was better? Which one would actually help her reach her goal?

She decided to run her own experiment.

Two Paths, One Goal

Emily took $500 from her savings and split it.

She put $250 into a **secured credit card** through her credit union. It was simple: she deposited the money, got a card with a $250 limit, and promised herself she'd only use it for gas.

Then she signed up for a **credit builder account**. For $25 a month, she'd make "payments" toward a locked savings account, and those payments would be reported as on-time installments to all three bureaus. After 12 months, she'd get her money back—plus interest.

She created two folders in her planner:

1. **Secured Card**
2. **Credit Builder**

Each month, she tracked payments, balances, and changes to her score. She even added alerts on her phone:

- "Pay secured card in full before statement date."
- "Credit builder payment due—auto-pay on."
- "Check credit score update."

She took it seriously. This was her financial comeback story, and she was documenting every step.

Three Months In

By month three, Emily started seeing results.

Her secured card was helping her with **revolving credit**—the type that affects your credit utilization. She always kept her balance below 10%, usually no more than $20 at a time. Her score jumped 34 points in the first 60 days.

Her credit builder account was reporting as an **installment loan**—which helped with her credit mix and payment history. It wasn't as dramatic, but it was steady. Ten more points added to her score by the third month.

She realized both tools were working—but in different ways.

The Difference That Matters

Emily also noticed something important:

- The **secured card** required discipline. If she spent too much or paid late, her score could drop quickly.
- The **credit builder account** was more automated. Payments were fixed, predictable, and reported like clockwork.

Each had its pros and cons.

Secured Card Pros:

- Immediate access to a credit line
- Builds utilization history

- Can eventually graduate to an unsecured card

Cons:

- Requires self-control
- Late payments hurt quickly
- Interest charges if you carry a balance

Credit Builder Account Pros:

- Builds payment history automatically
- Adds installment credit to your profile
- Helps you save money at the same time

Cons:

- No access to funds until end of term
- May take longer to impact score
- Doesn't help with utilization

By month five, Emily's score had risen to **673**—a 68-point improvement from where she started. That was enough to qualify for an auto loan with decent terms.

She walked into the dealership confident, not desperate. And when the finance officer looked at her credit report, he raised his eyebrows.

"You've got a solid credit mix for someone with a short history. Installment and revolving? Nicely done."

Emily smiled. Her experiment had paid off.

Emily's Takeaway: Use Both if You Can

If she had to choose only one, Emily said she'd start with a credit builder account. It was safer and helped her form consistent habits.

But combining both gave her the best results.

Here's What You Can Do Now:

1. **If you have savings to spare,** open a secured card with a low limit.
2. **If you prefer automation and saving,** open a credit builder account.
3. **If possible, do both.** One helps your utilization. The other improves your payment history and mix.
4. **Track everything monthly** and set alerts to avoid missing payments.

Remember: These tools are stepping stones—not lifelong accounts. The goal is to graduate to higher credit and better terms. Once your score improves, you'll qualify for unsecured cards and loans on your terms.

In the next chapter, we'll explore exactly how to **track and optimize your credit growth**, so you know when to take action and when to just stay consistent.

Because building credit without debt is one thing—but building it strategically? That's how you stay in control for life.

CHAPTER 7: HOW TO TRACK AND OPTIMIZE YOUR CREDIT GROWTH

If you've made it this far, you've already taken powerful action—activating rent reporting, using subscriptions, opening secured cards or builder accounts. Now it's time to shift from *building* mode to *optimization* mode.

This chapter is all about making sure your credit keeps growing—and doing it efficiently, without guessing.

Step 1: Monitor Your Credit Monthly

To track progress, you need visibility. Fortunately, you don't need to pay for it.

Use these free credit monitoring tools:

- **Credit Karma** (TransUnion & Equifax)
- **Experian.com** (includes free monthly FICO updates)
- **Credit Sesame**
- **NerdWallet**

These platforms allow you to:

- See your score change over time
- Check your credit report for errors

- Monitor utilization and payment history
- Get alerts for new activity or potential fraud

Set a reminder: Check once per month, not every day. Credit changes are slow and steady.

Step 2: Track Key Credit Score Factors

There are five key categories that make up your score. Track and optimize these like a credit professional:

1. **Payment History (35%)**
   - Pay all bills before the due date.
   - Automate payments to avoid human error.
   - Never miss even a $5 payment—it all counts.
2. **Credit Utilization (30%)**
   - Keep your credit card balances below 10% of your total limits.
   - If you can't pay off the full balance early, at least pay it *before the statement closing date*, not just the due date.
3. **Credit Age (15%)**

- Don't close your oldest accounts unless absolutely necessary.
- The longer your average age of accounts, the better.

4. **Credit Mix (10%)**
   - Include both revolving (credit cards) and installment (credit builder loans or auto loans) accounts.
   - You don't need many—just 1–2 of each type is enough.

5. **New Credit Inquiries (10%)**
   - Avoid applying for too many accounts in a short time.
   - Hard inquiries stay on your report for 2 years but only affect your score for about 6–12 months.

Step 3: Use a Credit Tracker or Spreadsheet

Keeping notes will help you stay focused and motivated.

Here's what to include:

Date	Credit Score	Credit Limit	Card	Balance	Utilization %	On-Time Payments
Jan 1	580	$300		$20	6%	yes
Feb 1	610	$300		$15	5%	yes
Mar 1	635	$300		$0	0%	yes

You can create this in Excel, Google Sheets, or even a notebook.

Bonus Tip: Some credit apps like Credit Karma or NerdWallet let you track this data visually with graphs.

Step 4: Set Milestone Goals (30-60-90 Days)

Credit growth takes time, but it helps to break it into realistic phases.

30-Day Goal:

- All accounts reporting on time
- Utilization below 10%
- Enrolled in credit monitoring

60-Day Goal:

- Score improves by 20–40 points
- No new hard inquiries
- Automated payments set for all accounts

90-Day Goal:

- Score increases by 50–100 points (if starting from no or low credit)
- Qualify for unsecured credit or better financial products
- Create a plan to graduate or close starter accounts responsibly

Step 5: Avoid These Optimization Mistakes

1. **Paying after the due date but before interest hits**
    - This still risks a late mark. Always pay before the due date.
2. **Maxing out cards and paying off after**
    - Utilization is reported on the *statement date*, not the due date. Keep balances low *before* the statement closes.
3. **Opening too many accounts at once**

  - Every hard inquiry costs you points short-term. Open only what's necessary.

4. **Closing starter accounts too early**
   - Keep your first credit accounts open unless there are annual fees or downsides. Age matters.

5. **Ignoring your credit report**
   - Errors happen. Dispute inaccurate info through AnnualCreditReport.com or directly with the bureaus.

Final Thoughts

Building credit is one thing. **Optimizing** it is what gets you to the next level—better rates, better terms, more opportunity.

Consistency is your best friend. Stay automated, stay informed, and celebrate small wins.

In the next chapter, we'll shift focus to something just as important: **How to stay debt-free while your credit continues to grow fast.** Because growth means nothing if it comes with risk—and your financial foundation should always feel stable.

How to Track and Optimize Your Credit Growth

Leah had always been one of those people who avoided credit entirely.

She grew up watching her parents argue about bills—past-due notices taped to the fridge, credit cards with maxed-out balances, and loan officers calling during dinner. So when she moved out on her own at 19, Leah made a vow: no credit, no debt, no drama.

For a while, it worked. She paid for everything in cash, never owed anyone, and didn't even think about her credit score. But then she hit a wall.

At 26, she applied to rent a small house near her new job as a dental assistant. The landlord smiled as she handed over her application—until he ran her credit.

"You don't really... exist," he said gently. "No score. No history. Nothing to evaluate."

Leah was stunned. "But I always pay on time! I don't have debt. Doesn't that mean I'm responsible?"

The landlord shrugged. "It means you're responsible—but it doesn't mean you're creditworthy. At least not in the system's eyes."

That night, Leah sat on her bed, staring at her laptop and wondering how to play this game she never wanted to join.

She didn't want credit for a fancy car or a shopping spree—she just wanted options. A place to live. A way to grow her future without being shut out.

So she made a new vow—not to avoid credit, but to master it on her terms.

The Tracking Begins

Leah opened a free account with Credit Karma and was greeted with the words: "No credit file found." But she also found tools—ones that could help her track every detail going forward.

She ordered her reports from all three bureaus through AnnualCreditReport.com. Blank slates. Not good, not bad—just... empty.

She didn't panic. She created a notebook titled **"Credit Growth Journal"** and wrote on the first page:
Day 1: From Invisible to Unstoppable.

Her first move was to sign up for a secured credit card. She used $300 from her savings and vowed to keep spending under $30 a month. She also activated a rent reporting service that added her monthly rent to her file—and looked into Experian Boost to add her phone and Netflix payments.

Every tool she used, she tracked in her journal:

- Credit Card Balance
- Credit Limit
- Payment Date
- Statement Closing Date
- Rent Reported: Yes
- Utilities Linked: Yes

She even color-coded it like a scrapbook.

Then she set up weekly reminders on her phone:

> "Check credit utilization."
> "Pay off secured card."
> "Log score update."

The First Score

It took about six weeks, but one day, the notification came through.

Your credit score has been updated: 623.

Leah nearly cried. It was a number—just a number—but it meant she existed in the system. Her rent, her bills, her $300 card—they were finally being recognized.

She flipped open her notebook and wrote:
"623. Progress. Proof. Potential."

From that moment on, she became obsessed—not with the score itself, but with understanding *how* it moved.

She noticed that if she paid off her card before the **statement date**, her utilization stayed low and her score climbed faster. When she accidentally let a $120 charge report one month, her score dropped 11 points—even though she paid it off before the due date.

That's when she learned: the **statement date** is more important than the **due date** when it comes to utilization reporting.

She also saw her **credit mix** improve after she opened a credit builder loan—her profile now showed both revolving (credit card) and installment (loan) accounts.

Every time her score moved, she logged the reason why.

From Passive to Proactive

After three months of tracking, Leah had it down to a science:

- She used **less than 10%** of her limit.
- She paid **three days before the statement date**.
- She checked all reports monthly for errors.
- She avoided **hard inquiries** like the plague.
- She didn't open any new accounts unless absolutely necessary.
- She had **auto-pay** set up for every bill.

Her score? **684** and climbing.

Leah knew people with more income and flashier lives who had worse credit than she did. The difference wasn't money—it was strategy.

What started as a panic-driven mission had turned into something empowering.

She was no longer afraid of credit—she respected it. Managed it. Used it.

The Bigger Picture

Leah didn't need a 750 to feel successful. But one day, she got pre-approved for a new apartment—no cosigner, no hassle. She moved into a sunlit studio that overlooked a small park. It wasn't fancy, but it was hers—and she earned it.

She taped a new piece of paper to her fridge:

"684: Built Without Debt. Managed With Discipline."

Then, underneath it, she added a second line:

"Goal: 720 by next summer."

And this time, she knew exactly how to get there.

CHAPTER 8: STAYING DEBT-FREE WHILE SCALING CREDIT FAST

Building credit is important—but staying debt-free while doing it? That's real power.

Too many people fall into the trap of chasing higher scores and better credit cards, only to end up buried in balances, minimum payments, and long-term financial stress. The good news is that you don't need debt to grow your credit—you just need smart strategy and consistent discipline.

This chapter will show you exactly how to scale your credit score fast without falling into the debt trap.

Step 1: Understand the Role of Credit Activity (Not Credit Use)

The credit system rewards **responsible activity**, not borrowing. You don't need to carry a balance or go into debt to grow your score.

Here's what counts:

- On-time payments
- Low credit utilization
- Age of accounts
- Account variety
- Responsible account management

"You don't get bonus points for paying interest."

In fact, carrying a balance hurts your score and your finances. The key is to show you can access credit—but choose not to use much of it.

Step 2: Automate Everything You Can

Automation removes the risk of human error. It's one of the best ways to stay debt-free while building a strong credit file.

Here's how:

- **Autopay the minimum** on every credit card or loan
- Set a **manual reminder** to pay the full balance early (before statement date if possible)
- Automate rent, utilities, and subscription payments from a separate account used only for bills

If your bills are automated, your credit score becomes automatic, too.

Step 3: Use the "1-1-1 Rule" for Smart Credit Card Management

If you want to use a credit card without falling into debt, follow this simple rule:

- Use **1 card** for 1 **type of purchase** (gas, groceries, etc.)
- Use **no more than 10%** of your limit
- Pay it off in full **1 week before the statement closing date**

This ensures:

- Low utilization
- No interest charges
- Positive monthly reporting

Example:
If your card limit is $500, never let your balance go above $50. If your statement closes on the 15th, pay it by the 8th—even if your due date is later.

Step 4: Gradually Increase Available Credit (Without Using It)

Higher limits improve your utilization ratio—but only if you don't increase your spending.

Here's how to raise your limit without increasing risk:

- After 3–6 months of on-time payments, request a credit limit increase
- Use language like "I'm building my credit profile and would like to increase my available credit without impacting my score."
- Don't use the new limit. Keep spending at the same low level.

Tip: Higher credit limits with low balances = better credit scores and stronger lending profiles.

Step 5: Use Credit Builder Tools That Don't Involve Loans

Avoid the temptation to "improve your mix" with unnecessary debt.

Instead, use:

- **Rent reporting services**
- **Experian Boost** (adds utilities and subscriptions)
- **Credit builder savings accounts** (like Self or CreditStrong)
- **Secured cards used for one bill only, paid in full monthly**

These tools build your credit without any risk of revolving debt, compound interest, or impulse purchases.

Step 6: Avoid the "Upgrade Trap"

As your score grows, you'll get offers: unsecured cards, higher limits, even loans or buy-now-pay-later programs. These can be tempting—but dangerous.

Before accepting any upgrade:

- Ask: Will this help my credit profile or tempt me to spend?
- Only accept if it improves your terms (lower APR, no fees) and you can control your usage

- Don't accept cards with rewards that lead to overspending ("Spend $1,000 to earn $50" is a trap)

Smart tip: Keep older, stable accounts open even if you don't use them. They strengthen your average age of credit.

Step 7: Create a "No-Debt Spending Plan"

Credit cards are not emergency funds.

If you're building credit while staying debt-free, you need a cash system that prevents credit reliance.

Create three buckets:

1. **Bills Account** (all automated payments)
2. **Spending Account** (daily expenses)
3. **Emergency Savings** (3–6 months of expenses)

Use your credit card for one fixed item (like your phone bill), and make sure your checking account has the cash to pay it off before it's due.

Step 8: Use Your Score Strategically, Not Emotionally

Your credit score is not a trophy—it's a tool.

Use it to:

- Qualify for apartments or housing with no cosigner

- Refinance high-interest loans if needed
- Open business accounts or utilities without deposits
- Lower your insurance premiums

"Don't use it to justify a lifestyle upgrade or unnecessary spending."

Step 9: Celebrate Milestones—Not Credit Limits

Your score will rise. You'll get offers. But the real win is staying in control.

Celebrate:

- Paying every bill on time for 12 months
- Hitting 700+ without carrying a balance
- Using your credit report to secure better opportunities—not more liabilities

Final Words

Scaling your credit is like building muscle—it happens with consistent, controlled reps. Not with big, risky lifts.

You can build a 750+ credit score without ever carrying a balance, paying a cent of interest, or taking out a loan you don't need. You just need the right plan—and the discipline to follow it.

In the next chapter, we'll look at **the most common mistakes that sabotage credit—and how to avoid them completely.**

Because as your score rises, the risks of missteps grow. But with knowledge and awareness, you can stay one step ahead.

Staying Debt-Free While Scaling Credit Fast

Jonah wasn't new to credit—he was new to using it wisely.

At 24, he'd already made the same mistake millions of people make: thinking a high credit limit meant he could afford more. His first credit card had a $1,000 limit. Within a few weeks, it had a $940 balance.

He promised himself he'd pay it off quickly. Then came an unexpected car repair. Then a missed day of work. Then an interest charge. The snowball started rolling.

Within six months, Jonah had three maxed-out cards and no idea how he'd dig himself out.

By the time he turned 25, he'd paid off most of it through sheer discipline—but his score was wrecked, and his confidence was low. That's when he made a new decision:

> "I'm going to rebuild my credit—but I'm not going back into debt to do it."

He opened a blank journal, titled the first page **"Credit Comeback—No Debt Required,"** and made a promise to himself: *I will grow my credit score without owing a single cent of interest again.*

The Turning Point

Jonah started by canceling all unnecessary subscriptions and building an emergency fund—even if it was just $50 a month. Then, he applied for a secured credit card with a $300 deposit and created a rule:

- Only one charge per month
- Never more than $25
- Pay in full a week before the statement date

He stuck to it like religion.

He called it his "Credit Gym"—small, consistent reps that would make his score stronger without straining his finances.

His friends didn't get it. "Dude, why not just use it for everything and rack up rewards?"

Jonah shook his head. "Because I know how this ends. This card isn't a reward. It's a report card. And I'm not failing again."

The System That Changed Everything

Jonah set up a three-account system:

1. **Bills Account:** Rent, utilities, phone, and the secured card auto-pay came from this.
2. **Spending Account:** Groceries, gas, and day-to-day expenses came from here.

3. **Emergency Savings:** Even if it was small, it was untouchable.

He also set alarms in his phone:

- **Day 7:** Check balance, pay off secured card.
- **Day 10:** Review credit reports.
- **Day 15:** Log credit score.

Each month, he tracked:

- Total credit limit
- Current utilization
- On-time payment streak
- Credit score progress

The funny thing was... the more he tracked, the less he worried. He wasn't guessing anymore. He was managing.

Staying the Course

Jonah's turning point came at the six-month mark. His credit score had climbed from 582 to 702.

He got letters in the mail: pre-approvals, loan offers, cash advance checks.

One night, he got a call from a car dealership.

> "Mr. Diaz, based on your new credit score, we can offer you $20,000 financing—no money down."

He almost said yes. His current car was old, loud, and barely hanging on. The offer was tempting.

But he thought back to that journal entry: *No debt required.*

He thanked them politely and hung up the phone.
Then he made a new journal entry:
"Today I said no to temptation—and yes to my future."

The Real Victory

Jonah didn't buy the car. Instead, he saved $1,000 and bought a reliable used one outright. He kept using his secured card for Spotify and gas. He never carried a balance. Never paid a cent in interest.

By the time he hit his one-year credit comeback anniversary, he was sitting at a 745 credit score.

More importantly, he had peace of mind. No late payments. No minimums. No balance anxiety.

He started coaching his younger brother on how to build credit smart—and became the go-to guy at work for financial advice.

> "You don't need debt to win the credit game," he told people. "You just need discipline, a system, and a reason."

For Jonah, that reason was freedom. Not just from bad credit—but from the stress that came with it.

What Jonah Taught Us

Jonah proved what this chapter is all about:

- You can scale your credit score without debt.
- You don't need to carry balances or open new loans.
- The key is to use credit like a tool, not a temptation.

Because in the end, credit is about *control*. And when you own the system—without letting it own you—that's when you truly win.

CHAPTER 9: COMMON MISTAKES THAT SABOTAGE CREDIT

You've learned how to build credit without borrowing, how to track your progress, and how to stay debt-free. But even the most careful people can stumble into mistakes that undo all their hard work.

In this chapter, we'll cover the most common credit mistakes—what they are, why they happen, and exactly how to avoid them.

Mistake #1: Carrying a Balance Thinking It Helps

The Myth: You need to carry a balance to improve your credit score.
The Truth: Carrying a balance costs you money and lowers your score.

Why it happens: Many people confuse "using credit" with "owing money." But credit bureaus reward *activity*, not *debt*.

How to avoid it:

- Use your card for small purchases.
- Pay the balance in full before the statement closing date.
- Set alerts to pay weekly or biweekly.

Bottom Line: Carrying a balance doesn't help your score—it just earns banks interest.

Mistake #2: Paying Late (Even Once)

The Myth: One late payment isn't a big deal.
The Truth: A single late payment can drop your score by 50–100 points.

Why it happens: People forget due dates, misunderstand statement timing, or wait until the last minute.

How to avoid it:

- Set all bills on autopay for at least the minimum due.
- Use digital reminders to double-check due dates.
- Pay early—especially with credit cards.

Tip: Late payments stay on your credit report for up to 7 years. Protect your payment history at all costs.

Mistake #3: Ignoring Statement Dates vs. Due Dates

The Myth: As long as you pay by the due date, your credit report looks fine.
The Truth: Credit utilization is reported on the **statement closing date**, not the payment due date.

Why it happens: Most people assume payments are only about avoiding fees—not about how your score is calculated.

How to avoid it:

- Find out your card's statement closing date.
- Pay down your balance before this date, not just by the due date.
- Keep your reported balance under 10% of your total limit.

Example: If your limit is $500, keep your balance under $50 *before* the statement closes.

Mistake #4: Closing Old Accounts

The Myth: Closing unused cards is smart because it reduces temptation.
The Truth: Closing accounts can hurt your credit age and increase utilization.

Why it happens: People want to simplify their finances, cut up cards, or avoid fees.

How to avoid it:

- Keep old cards open unless they charge an annual fee.
- Use them for small purchases once every 3–6 months to keep them active.
- If you must close a card, close the *newest* one, not the oldest.

Tip: Your oldest accounts build your "credit age," which impacts up to 15% of your score.

Mistake #5: Applying for Too Many Accounts Too Quickly

The Myth: More cards mean faster credit building.
The Truth: Multiple hard inquiries in a short time signal risk.

Why it happens: People get excited by pre-approval offers or want to jump from 0 to 750 overnight.

How to avoid it:

- Space out applications by 3–6 months.
- Only apply when absolutely necessary.
- Avoid store credit cards that offer "discounts today" in exchange for new inquiries.

Tip: Hard inquiries stay on your report for 2 years but affect your score most in the first 6–12 months.

Mistake #6: Letting Small Bills Go to Collections

The Myth: A $50 bill doesn't matter if you forget it.
The Truth: A $50 collections account can drop your score like a rock.

Why it happens: People overlook old medical bills, parking tickets, or forgotten utilities when moving.

How to avoid it:

- Check your credit report quarterly for unexpected collections.
- Set mail forwarding and close accounts when moving.
- Contact companies before an account goes past due.

Tip: Paid collections may still show on your report, but newer scoring models weigh them less—especially medical debt.

Mistake #7: Misunderstanding Utilization on Multiple Cards

The Myth: As long as your *total* usage is low, you're fine.
The Truth: Each card's utilization is measured *individually* and can affect your score.

Why it happens: People track overall usage but ignore maxed-out individual cards.

How to avoid it:

- Keep each card below 30%, ideally under 10%.
- If one card is maxed, pay it down even if others have zero balances.
- Use balance reminders or apps to monitor usage in real-time.

Mistake #8: Not Reviewing Your Credit Reports Regularly

The Myth: Your credit report is fine if your score looks good.
The Truth: Errors, fraud, or outdated information can hurt your score quietly.

Why it happens: Credit reports are long, complicated, and easy to ignore.

How to avoid it:

- Check your credit report from all 3 bureaus every 3–6 months.
- Use AnnualCreditReport.com for free access.
- Dispute inaccuracies directly with bureaus online.

Look for:

- Incorrect late payments
- Accounts you don't recognize
- Outdated or duplicated information

Mistake #9: Relying Too Much on Credit to Get By

The Myth: Using credit to "float" until payday is harmless.
The Truth: This can lead to a slow debt spiral and missed payments.

Why it happens: Life gets expensive—and credit seems easier than budgeting.

How to avoid it:

- Build a buffer of 1 month's expenses (even if slowly).
- Use your credit card for things you can pay off immediately.
- Treat credit like a tool—not a solution for emergencies.

Final Words

Avoiding these mistakes isn't about being perfect—it's about being **proactive**.

Credit success isn't just built by what you do—it's protected by what you *don't* do. And once you understand these traps, you'll be able to sidestep them for life.

In the next chapter, we'll take everything you've learned and apply it with purpose. You'll learn how to create **30-day, 60-day, and 90-day credit growth plans** to hit your target score—fast, safe, and debt-free.

Common Mistakes That Sabotage Credit

Angela was the first in her family to have "good credit."

After rebuilding her score from the low 500s to a proud 712 over the course of a year, she felt unstoppable. She had a secured card, a credit builder loan, and even a rent reporting service. She followed every tip, paid everything on time, and tracked her progress like a pro.

One Friday afternoon, she sat in her car outside a clothing store, looking at a "You're Pre-Approved!" email on her phone from a retail brand she liked.

"$1,000 credit limit. 20% off your purchase today."

It seemed harmless. She had worked so hard—maybe she deserved to reward herself. Besides, she wouldn't go overboard.

Angela opened the account, got her discount, and bought $250 worth of clothes. She felt a little guilty—but it was still under the limit. What she didn't know was that the card's statement closed five days later—and reported the $250 balance to the credit bureaus.

The Score Drops

The following month, Angela logged into Credit Karma, ready to see another jump.

Instead, her jaw dropped:
Score: 679.

"What?" she gasped. "How did I lose 33 points?"

She scrolled through her report, confused. The payments were still on time. Nothing was in collections. Then she spotted it: the new store card. A $250 balance on a $1,000 limit = 25% utilization. Not terrible—but added to her other small balances, her overall utilization was now above 30%.

It didn't help that her new account also triggered a **hard inquiry**, and her **average age of credit** had dropped from 2 years to 1.5 years.

She was furious—not at the store, but at herself.

"I worked so hard to build this," she muttered. "And I messed it up in a single afternoon."

The Snowball Begins

Angela vowed to fix it quickly. But things got worse before they got better.

The next month, she forgot to pay her secured card *before* the statement closed. It reported a $180 balance on a $300 limit—60% utilization.

Then, she paid her phone bill two days late. Not because she couldn't afford it, but because she thought the autopay was set up—it wasn't.

The result?

Score: 648.

In two months, she lost nearly 65 points.

Angela sat on her couch one night, staring at her planner, tears of frustration forming in her eyes.

> "I didn't max out cards... I didn't miss a loan payment. How did this happen?"

The Turnaround

Determined not to fall back into old habits, Angela decided to start fresh—this time not just building credit, but *protecting* it.

She bought a small whiteboard and wrote in bold letters:
"Credit Safety = Credit Success"

She made a new checklist:

- Don't apply for anything unless it's essential
- Never let a balance exceed 10% of a card limit
- Always check due dates vs. statement dates
- Automate everything—but verify autopay setups
- Pay early—never just on time
- Monitor credit every month—watch for errors, spikes, or new accounts

Angela then called the store card company and paid off the balance. She didn't close the card—she just vowed never to use it again.

Next, she set calendar reminders for every statement closing date. No more late payments. No more balance surprises.

And she gave herself one more rule:
No emotional spending. Credit is for control—not comfort.

The Climb Back Up

Three months later, Angela's score crept back to 692. Not where it was—but getting close.

More importantly, she felt like she had grown. Credit wasn't just numbers on a screen. It was a reflection of habits, awareness, and self-control.

Her cousin asked for help one weekend. "I'm trying to build my score—what should I do?"

Angela smiled.

> "I'll tell you what to do—but I'll also tell you what *not* to do. Because avoiding mistakes is half the battle."

She handed her cousin a notebook and wrote on the first page:
"Don't build a credit score you can't protect."

Angela's Lessons Learned

Angela's story reminds us of what every listener needs to hear:

- A few small mistakes can trigger big score drops.
- Emotional spending or chasing perks can lead to unnecessary inquiries and poor utilization.
- Ignoring statement dates and automation errors can undo months of progress.
- The real power isn't in building a high score—it's in maintaining it through consistency.

Now, she still has great credit. But she's not chasing perfection—she's chasing stability.

And she's helping others do the same.

CHAPTER 10: YOUR 30-DAY, 60-DAY, AND 90-DAY CREDIT GROWTH PLANS

If you've followed everything up to this point, you're ready to take powerful, focused action. This chapter is your 3-phase blueprint to build and scale your credit score over the next 90 days—**without borrowing money or going into debt**.

These step-by-step plans will help you:

- Organize your efforts
- Prioritize high-impact actions
- Stay consistent without burnout
- See real, measurable results

Let's break it down by time frame:

Phase 1: The 30-Day Credit Foundation Plan

Goal: Establish a credit footprint and get your first score or a solid point boost.

Week 1: Activate Your Credit Visibility

- **Pull your credit reports** from all 3 bureaus at AnnualCreditReport.com.
- **Sign up for credit monitoring tools** like Credit Karma, Experian, or NerdWallet.

- Note what's on your reports: open accounts, balances, payment history, collections, etc.

Week 2: Add Low-Risk Reporting Accounts

- Sign up for **rent reporting services** (Boom, RentReporters, or LevelCredit).
- Enroll in **Experian Boost** to add phone, utility, and streaming payments.
- Open a **secured credit card** with a deposit of $200–$300, but only use it for one essential bill (like gas or a phone plan).

Week 3: Automate and Optimize

- **Set up autopay** for all bills—credit card, rent, subscriptions, and utilities.
- **Note your credit card's statement closing date** (not just the due date).
- Create a system to pay off your balance 3–5 days *before* the statement closes.

Week 4: Build Your Credit Habits

- Track your credit activity in a spreadsheet or notebook:
    - Utilization %

   - On-time payment status
   - Alerts for due and statement dates

- Avoid applying for any more accounts or loans.

Expected Results:

- Your first score if you had none
- +20 to +40 point boost if you had a thin file
- Clean foundation to build stronger activity in the next 60 days

Phase 2: The 60-Day Credit Acceleration Plan

Goal: Strengthen credit activity, improve utilization, and raise your score more significantly.

Week 5–6: Maintain and Monitor

- Keep secured card spending below **10%** of the credit limit.
- Continue tracking rent and utility payments.
- Log in to your credit monitoring tool weekly to watch for:
   - Score changes
   - Utilization alerts

- Payment history updates

Week 7–8: Strengthen Credit Mix

- If you haven't already, open a **credit builder savings account** (like Self or CreditStrong).
  - These report as installment loans and help diversify your credit profile.
- Make the monthly payment automatic (as little as $25/month).
- Do **not** open any new revolving credit cards unless necessary.

Week 9: Request a Credit Limit Increase

- If your secured card issuer allows it, request a small credit limit increase.
- You can say:

"I'm building my credit history responsibly and would like to increase my available credit to improve my utilization ratio."

- Some issuers will raise your limit without a hard inquiry.

Week 10–12: Clean Up and Consolidate

- Review your credit report for any errors or duplicate accounts.
- Dispute incorrect information directly with the bureaus.
- Check that old collections, if any, are either settled or validated.

Expected Results:

- +40 to +70 point increase, depending on previous activity
- Improved credit mix (installment + revolving)
- More robust credit history with stable reporting

Phase 3: The 90-Day Credit Optimization Plan

Goal: Solidify gains, lower risk indicators, and qualify for better credit products.

Week 13–14: Optimize Utilization Ratios

- If you've received a credit limit increase, **recalculate your new utilization** and keep spending under 10%.
- Pay balances early—not just in full, but before the **statement date**, to keep low balances reported.

- If you have multiple cards, keep each individual card below 10% as well—not just the total.

Week 15: Assess Credit Opportunities (Cautiously)

- Check if you're prequalified (soft pull only) for:
    - An unsecured card with no annual fee
    - A student or beginner rewards card
- If and only if you're above 680, consider upgrading—but avoid store cards or offers that require spending minimums.

Week 16–17: Lock in Positive Behavior

- Maintain 100% on-time payments
- Keep all accounts active with light usage
- Avoid new credit applications

Week 18–19: Plan Your Next Quarter

- Set a new 90-day goal (e.g., hit 720+, refinance auto loan, qualify for a better rental).
- Decide which cards or accounts you'll continue using long-term—and which to keep open just for credit age and utilization.

Expected Results:

- +70 to +120 point total gain (if starting low or thin)
- Pre-approval for credit cards, apartment leases, or low-limit financing
- Sustainable, automated credit system you can use for life

Additional Tips for All 3 Phases

- **Journal Your Progress:** Writing down small wins keeps you motivated.
- **Create a Visual Tracker:** Use a chart or app to monitor score changes, card usage, and milestones.
- **Focus on Behavior, Not Score:** The score will follow if the behavior stays strong.

Your 30-Day, 60-Day, and 90-Day Credit Growth Plans

The day Eric was denied for a used car loan, he felt like someone had punched him in the gut.

He wasn't trying to buy anything fancy—just a reliable car so he could stop taking three buses to work. He had a steady job as a pharmacy tech, a modest income, and a clean history.

But the bank didn't care about that.

> "We can't approve this application. Your credit score is too low, and you don't have enough credit activity."

Eric walked out of that office embarrassed—and angry.

Not because he'd done anything wrong. But because **he hadn't done anything** at all. No missed payments, no debt, no credit cards. Just no *history.*

That's when he made a decision:

> "I'm giving myself 90 days to fix this."

Phase One: The 30-Day Foundation

Eric went home that night and started his plan.
He wrote across the top of a blank sheet of paper:
Day 1 – Credit Comeback Plan

He ordered all three credit reports from AnnualCreditReport.com. What he saw was... basically nothing. Just an old utility account marked paid and a student account that had closed.

He downloaded Credit Karma and Experian, and created a spreadsheet to track:

- Payment history
- Credit usage
- Score updates
- Action items

By Day 3, he had opened a **secured credit card** with a $300 deposit and linked it to just one monthly bill: his cell phone.

Then he found a **rent reporting service**, which allowed him to report 12 months of on-time rent payments. Within two weeks, he was finally on the map.

His score appeared: **612.**
Not amazing—but he existed.

He set calendar reminders for everything:

- Pay off the card on the 10th (before statement date on the 13th)
- Check credit score every 30 days
- Avoid using more than $30 per month on the card

He stuck to it religiously.

Phase Two: The 60-Day Acceleration

By week 5, Eric's score was up to **637**. Small jump—but it was progress.

He didn't apply for anything new. Instead, he added a **credit builder account** through Self. For $25 a month, it would report as an installment loan—helping with his credit mix.

He didn't touch the secured card except for phone bills and gas. Always under $30. Always paid early.

Around week 7, he called his card issuer and politely asked:

> "I've been using my card responsibly. Is it possible to increase my limit?"

They bumped it from $300 to $500 without a hard inquiry.

He didn't spend a penny more—but now his utilization dropped from 10% to 6%.

By week 8, his score hit **668.**

Eric felt like a credit ninja.

Phase Three: The 90-Day Optimization

In month three, Eric went into "maintenance mode."
No new accounts. No overspending. No skipped payments.

He opened a second checking account—just for bills—so there was never a missed payment or overdrawn account. He turned off unnecessary subscriptions and kept his financial life simple.

One day, he got a pre-approval email from a major credit card company.
"$1,500 limit, no annual fee, reward points."

He read the fine print. No hard pull. No gimmicks.

But he passed on it.

> "I'm not here to flex—I'm here to fix," he reminded himself.

Instead, he logged his progress and reviewed his goals:

- No debt
- Keep utilization under 10%

- Score over 680 by Day 90

Day 90: The Payoff

On Day 90, Eric opened Credit Karma and stared at the screen.

Score: 691.

He laughed out loud. He'd missed 700 by a sliver—but it didn't matter. He did it. He had built a solid credit score from scratch, with no loans, no late payments, and not a single dollar of interest paid.

More than that—he'd built confidence.

He printed out his plan and put it in a folder labeled: **"Credit Playbook."** Then he wrote another line:
Next goal: 720 by summer.

Eric's Credit Growth Formula

- **Days 1–30:** Add secured card, report rent, automate payments
- **Days 31–60:** Add builder loan, request credit limit increase, keep usage low
- **Days 61–90:** Stop applying, keep accounts active, optimize timing and behavior

Three months ago, Eric was invisible in the credit world.

Now? He was one of the smartest guys in the room—and soon, he'd be one of the most qualified. The next time he walked into a bank, he wouldn't be asking for permission—he'd be showing them a credit report that said *he was ready*.

CHAPTER 11: REAL STORIES OF FAST CREDIT GROWTH WITHOUT LOANS

The path to strong credit doesn't have to run through debt, loans, or high interest rates. These three stories prove that with the right tools and a little commitment, anyone—no matter their age, income, or history—can build a powerful credit profile, completely debt-free.

Let's talk about Naomi for a moment.

Naomi was 32, recently divorced, and starting over in a new city with her two kids. She had always let her ex-husband handle the finances. Now she had to rebuild—on her own terms.

When she tried to lease an apartment in a better school district, the leasing office denied her.

> "Your score is too low, and there's just not enough on your report," the agent said.

Naomi had never missed rent, paid every utility on time, and had a steady job. But none of that mattered because it wasn't *reported.*

Determined not to let her children down, Naomi did her research. Within a week, she signed up for:

- A **rent reporting service** that backdated 24 months of rent payments
- **Experian Boost**, linking her cell phone, electric, and Netflix bills

- A **secured credit card** with a $250 limit that she used only for groceries

She automated every payment, made a spreadsheet to track her progress, and committed to using less than 10% of her available credit. By the end of month one, she had a credit score—**from nothing to 631**.

Three months later, her score was **688**, and the same leasing office that turned her away now approved her with no cosigner.

Naomi didn't borrow a penny. She just leveraged the life she was already living—and made it reportable.

Now, let's talk about Marcus who went from 18 to 710 in 90 days

Marcus was 18 and ready to start his adult life the smart way. His uncle had struggled with bad credit for years, and Marcus was determined to avoid the same trap.

He had a part-time job, a checking account, and a prepaid phone—but no credit history.

Instead of waiting to be denied for his first apartment, Marcus took action early. He followed a strategy he found on a credit-building podcast and set up the following plan:

1. Opened a **Self credit builder account** at $25/month
2. Added his rent and internet through a reporting service
3. Opened a **secured credit card** with a $200 deposit

4. Used it once a week for gas and paid in full before the statement date

5. Tracked his score weekly and never let a single bill go unpaid

By the 30-day mark, he had a score of **645**. By Day 60, it was **682**. And by Day 90, Marcus celebrated his **710 score** with a modest secured credit card upgrade—and a new apartment lease approved on his own.

He had no loans. No debt. No interest payments. Just planning, patience, and discipline.

Let's quickly go over Priya's story now: Fixing What She Didn't Break

Priya was a nurse who had just moved from another country. Although she had years of perfect financial habits back home, her U.S. credit file was empty.

She applied for a credit card. Denied. Applied for a furniture financing offer. Denied again.

> "You have no history here," the rep told her. "You're considered a credit risk."

Priya was stunned. Back home, she had paid every bill early and never carried debt. But in the U.S., she was invisible.

She didn't want to take out a loan. So she found a strategy that worked:

- She signed up with **Nova Credit** to transfer some of her international credit history to Experian

- She added her **U.S. rental payments** and utilities using a rent reporting tool

- She got a **secured credit card** with a $500 deposit and used it to pay her hospital parking fees—just $3/day

She read about credit statement dates and never let a balance report over $40. After 60 days, her score popped up: **652**. Not great—but she existed.

By month three, Priya's score was **705**. She was approved for a better card, and when she applied to finance new appliances for her apartment, she was finally approved—with a smile.

No debt. No games. Just patience and systemization.

What These Stories Have in Common

These three people had different backgrounds and goals—but the same strategy:

- They **started with what they already had** (rent, phone bills, utilities)

- They **used secured cards wisely**

- They **never carried a balance**

- They **tracked their progress**
- They **avoided unnecessary applications**
- And most importantly, they **didn't borrow money to build credit**

Their results?

- Naomi: +100 points and a new apartment
- Marcus: 0 to 710 in 90 days
- Priya: No U.S. credit history to a 705 score in three months

The Big Takeaway

You don't need a bank loan, car loan, or thousands of dollars to build credit fast.

You need a plan.

And these stories prove it works.

In the final chapter, you'll get a powerful summary of everything you've learned—plus your next steps for continuing your credit journey without falling into debt.

CHAPTER 12: FINAL THOUGHTS & SUMMARY

Congratulations. If you've made it this far, you've done more than listen to a credit book—you've taken the first step in transforming your financial future, without falling into the trap of debt.

This final chapter will review the most powerful lessons from this journey, reinforce the habits that protect your score, and show you how to keep building credit safely for the rest of your life.

What You've Learned – The Credit Without Debt Framework

Let's recap the core ideas:

1. You Don't Need Debt to Build Credit

- You need **activity**, not balances.
- Credit scores reward consistency, not interest payments.

2. You Can Use What You Already Pay For

- Rent, subscriptions, and utility bills can be added to your credit profile.
- Services like **Boom**, **Experian Boost**, and **LevelCredit** make this easy.

3. Secured Credit Cards Are Your Friend—If Used Right

- Deposit-based cards offer safe revolving credit.
- Always keep balances below 10% and pay before the statement date.
- These are temporary tools—not permanent necessities.

4. Credit Builder Accounts Add Payment History

- Tools like **Self** and **CreditStrong** report installment loans without actual debt.
- Small monthly payments build your file and help diversify your credit mix.

5. Authorized User Accounts Provide a Head Start

- You can gain credit history from someone else's clean, long-standing card.
- Only use this with people you trust—and who have excellent credit habits.

The 90-Day Plan—Your Roadmap to Results

You also built (or are about to build) your credit using a 3-phase plan:

30 Days – The Foundation

- Open your first reporting accounts (rent, utilities, secured card)
- Start tracking and automating payments
- Create your credit calendar and budget

60 Days – The Acceleration

- Add a credit builder loan to strengthen your mix
- Request a credit limit increase if possible
- Maintain perfect payment history and low utilization

90 Days – The Optimization

- Keep all accounts active
- Avoid new applications unless necessary
- Review and clean up your credit report
- Set new long-term credit goals

Habits That Keep You Safe and Growing

These 10 habits will keep your score rising—and your financial stress low:

1. **Never carry a balance** if you can help it
2. **Pay before the statement date**, not just the due date
3. **Keep credit utilization under 10%**
4. **Review your reports quarterly** for errors
5. **Set all bills on autopay**—then check that they process
6. **Keep your oldest accounts open**, even if unused
7. **Avoid store cards** and rewards traps that encourage spending
8. **Don't apply for too many accounts too fast**
9. **Use credit tracking apps** and review score trends monthly
10. **Celebrate behavior, not the number**—score is a byproduct of discipline

How to Use Your New Credit Power

With a strong credit score, you now have access to:

- **Better housing options** without a cosigner
- **Lower security deposits** on utilities and rentals
- **Approval for credit cards** with rewards or travel points
- **Lower interest rates** if you *do* choose to finance something responsibly
- **Business and investment tools** like business credit cards and funding
- **Emergency peace of mind**—you're no longer financially invisible

Remember: credit isn't about spending—it's about **leverage**. You can now use credit to create more freedom and opportunity, not more stress.

Your Next Steps

Here's what to do after you finish this book:

1. **Review your current credit plan.** Update your goals.
2. **Decide which tools to keep, and which to phase out.**
    - For example: You may want to close a credit builder loan once completed, but keep a long-standing card active.

3. **Set a 6-month and 12-month credit goal.**
    - 6-month: Raise score by 40 points
    - 12-month: Qualify for a rewards card or refinance high-interest debt
4. **Keep tracking. Keep learning.** You've just unlocked a lifelong skillset.

Final Message

You've proven something powerful:
You don't need loans, debt, or a big income to win the credit game.

You just need:

- A strategy
- A system
- And a commitment to financial growth

Whether your goal is to buy a home, launch a business, travel, or simply never stress about money again—strong credit is your foundation. And now you know how to build it without borrowing a dime.

You've got this.
And your future is going to thank you.

EPILOGUE

If you've made it to this point, then you've already achieved what many people still believe is impossible: you've learned how to build real credit, fast, **without taking on debt**.

You didn't fall into the trap of high-interest loans.
You didn't rack up balances in the name of "credit activity."
You didn't rely on someone else to fix your credit for you.
You learned how to do it yourself.

That puts you in the top 10% of people who understand how the credit system really works. And more importantly, you've taken back control.

You're not invisible anymore.

Now, the financial system *knows your name*—and more importantly, it recognizes your behavior.

Maybe you started this audiobook unsure of your score—or unsure if you even had one. Maybe you've been denied in the past, or feared credit because of what it did to someone close to you.

But now you know better.

You've shifted your mindset from fear to strategy. You've turned your rent, your subscriptions, your small purchases, and your habits into credit-building tools. You've learned that credit isn't just for "other people." It's for **you**—and you can manage it on your own terms.

You've gone from wondering if you could qualify... to choosing what you'll qualify *for*.

That shift—from reaction to intention—is one of the most powerful changes you can make in your financial life.

So what now?

Now, you set new goals.

Do you want to:

- Lease a new apartment without a cosigner?
- Get approved for an unsecured credit card with rewards?
- Launch your own business and access capital?
- Buy your first home in a few years?

Whatever your next step is, your credit is ready to support you. All you have to do is continue the same smart habits you built over the last 90 days:

- Automate everything
- Keep utilization under 10%
- Pay before the statement date
- Avoid unnecessary applications
- Track your progress monthly
- Review your reports for errors
- Use credit as a tool—not a temptation

Keep it simple. Keep it steady. And stay in control.

There will be temptations ahead—rewards cards, financing offers, store promotions, and balance transfer games.

You don't need them.

The real power lies in *what you don't owe.* A 720 score that comes with no balances and no interest is worth more than an 800 score with $30,000 in revolving debt.

So guard your credit. Grow it slowly. And use it strategically.

You've proven that you can build credit **without borrowing**. That means you can now qualify for better products **without relying on them**.

You are not dependent. You are empowered.

And you've built a skillset that will last for life.

Most people never learn this.

They continue to believe the lies: that debt is necessary, that balance-carrying is smart, that good credit is only for high earners or people with perfect pasts.

You now know that's false.

So if you know someone struggling with credit, trying to get approved, or living in fear of their score—share this audiobook with them.

Give them the tools. Walk them through the steps. Or simply send them to the next book in the *Credit to Capital* series.

You never know who needs this knowledge. And you never know how much of a difference it can make in someone's life—just like it made in yours.

How to Build Credit Fast Without Debt was just one step in a larger journey.

In the rest of the *Credit to Capital* series, you'll learn how to:

- Repair bad credit and remove inaccuracies
- Build business credit without a personal guarantee
- Start a credit repair business to help others
- Use your credit to fund real estate and business ventures
- Turn personal credit into capital for long-term wealth

Because credit is just the beginning. What you do with it is where the real opportunity lies.

Thank you for trusting me to guide you through this journey. Your credit future is bright, strong, and **debt-free**.

Now go use it wisely.
And I'll see you in the next book.

— Joe Correa

CREDIT-BUILDING CHECKLIST (NO DEBT REQUIRED)

Goal: Build a strong credit score before graduation—without loans or interest.

Step 1: Establish a Credit Profile

☐ Check if you have a credit report at AnnualCreditReport.com
☐ Sign up for free credit monitoring (Credit Karma, Experian, NerdWallet)
☐ If no score appears, don't worry—it's normal at first

Step 2: Open Your First Credit Accounts

☐ Open a **secured credit card** (minimum $200 deposit)
☐ Use it for one fixed expense (e.g. gas, Spotify, groceries)
☐ Apply for a **credit builder loan** (e.g. through Self or CreditStrong)
☐ Enroll in **Experian Boost** to report phone and utility bills
☐ Use a **rent reporting service** if you're renting off-campus or with roommates

Step 3: Set Up Smart Payment Habits

☐ Put all bills on **autopay**
☐ Set reminders to **pay credit card before the statement date** (not just due date)

☐ Keep card usage **under 10% of your limit** (e.g., spend under $20 on a $200 card)

Step 4: Monitor & Track Your Progress

☐ Check your credit score monthly
☐ Track:
- Credit utilization
- On-time payments
- Age of accounts

☐ Keep your oldest account open—even if unused

Step 5: Avoid These Mistakes

☐ Don't apply for store credit cards or multiple accounts at once
☐ Don't close your first card after graduation (it helps your score grow)
☐ Don't carry a balance—**pay in full every month**
☐ Don't co-sign for others unless you're 100% certain of their responsibility

Credit Milestones to Aim For

☐ 1 month: Get your first score (600s+ range is common)
☐ 3 months: Reach 650–680 by using tools and tracking
☐ 6 months: Qualify for better cards or apartment rental approval
☐ 12 months: 700+ credit score with zero debt

FINAL WORD FROM THE AUTHOR

I've made it my mission to help people build credit the right way. I started with nothing. No guide, no mentor, no money. But once I learned the system, I realized something life-changing:

> "You don't need to go into debt to be powerful.
> You just need knowledge, structure, and action."

Now you have all three.

Stay consistent. Stay disciplined. And never forget—you are the one in control.

Thank you for listening.

If this book helped you understand how to build credit the smart way—without loans, debt, or confusion—then this is just the beginning.

Here's what to do next:

1. **Check out the other books on credit** and keep learning.
2. **Leave a review.**
   Your feedback helps others discover this book—and helps us create more content that supports your growth.

3. **Share this with someone who needs it.**
   A friend, a student, a family member—someone in your life may be struggling with credit, not because they're irresponsible, but because they've never been shown the right path.

You now know better—and you can help them do better.

Other Books in the *Credit to Capital* Series

By Joe Correa

Unlock the full financial journey with these powerful and practical books in the *Credit to Capital* series. Each volume is designed to help you build, repair, and leverage credit to create wealth, purchase property, and launch businesses—no matter where you're starting from.

- **Book 1: How to Establish Credit in the U.S.**
- **Book 2: Personal Credit Repair Blueprint**
- **Book 3: How to Build Credit Fast Without Debt**
- **Book 4: Business Credit Mastery**
- **Book 5: Credit Card Secrets for Building Wealth & Rewards**
- **Book 6: Credit Card Hacking for Smart Borrowers**
- **Book 7: How to Leverage Business Credit to Fund Real Estate Purchases**
- **Book 8: Business Credit Ecosystem: Build, Stack & Automate Unlimited Funding Without Personal Risk**
- **Book 9: How to Get $1M in Credit and Keep It**
- **Book 10: Credit-Funded Wealth for Families**

www.ingramcontent.com/pod-product-compliance
Ingram Content Group UK Ltd.
Pitfield, Milton Keynes, MK11 3LW, UK
UKHW021240300926
15471UKWH00014B/931

9 798349 558832